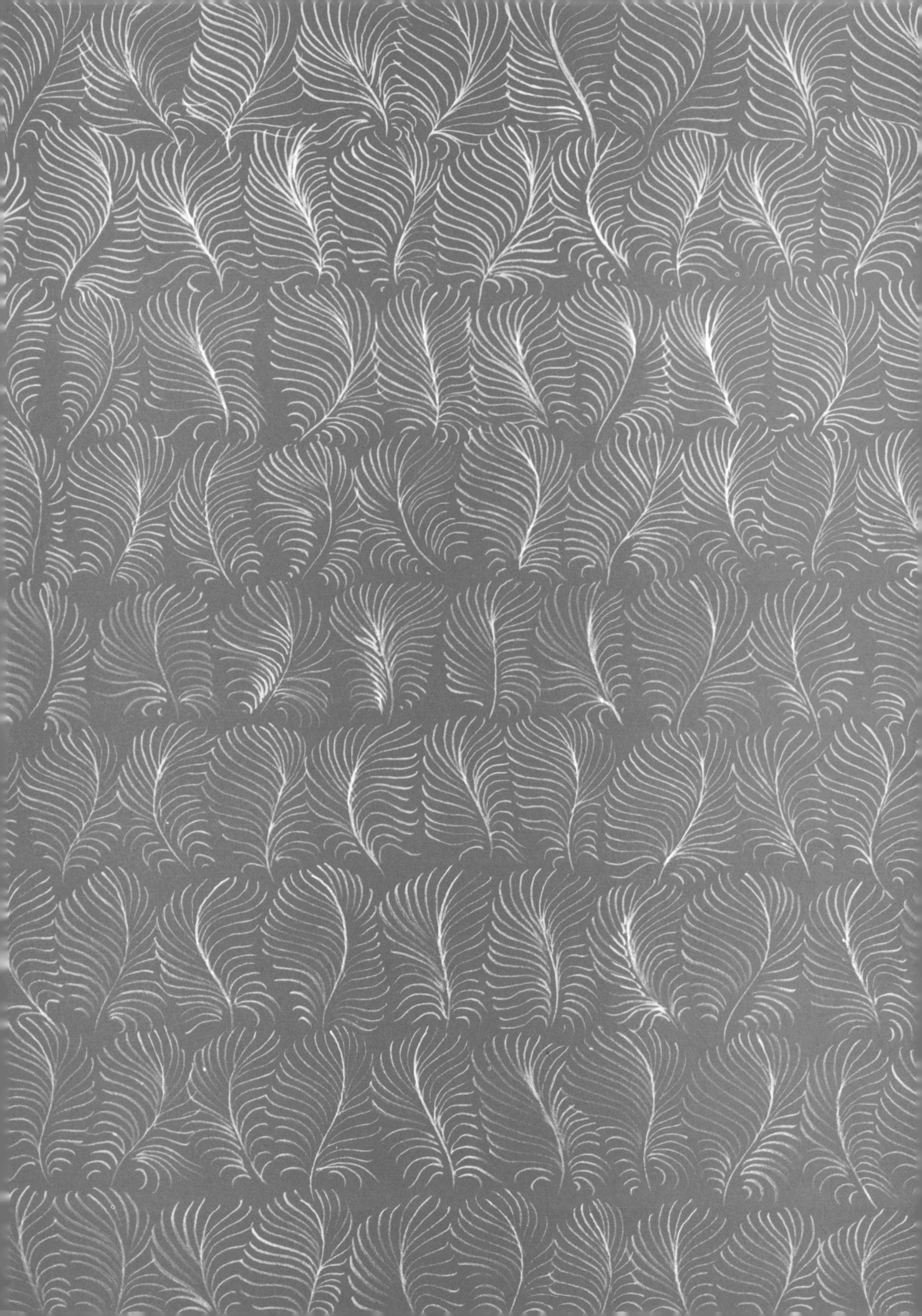

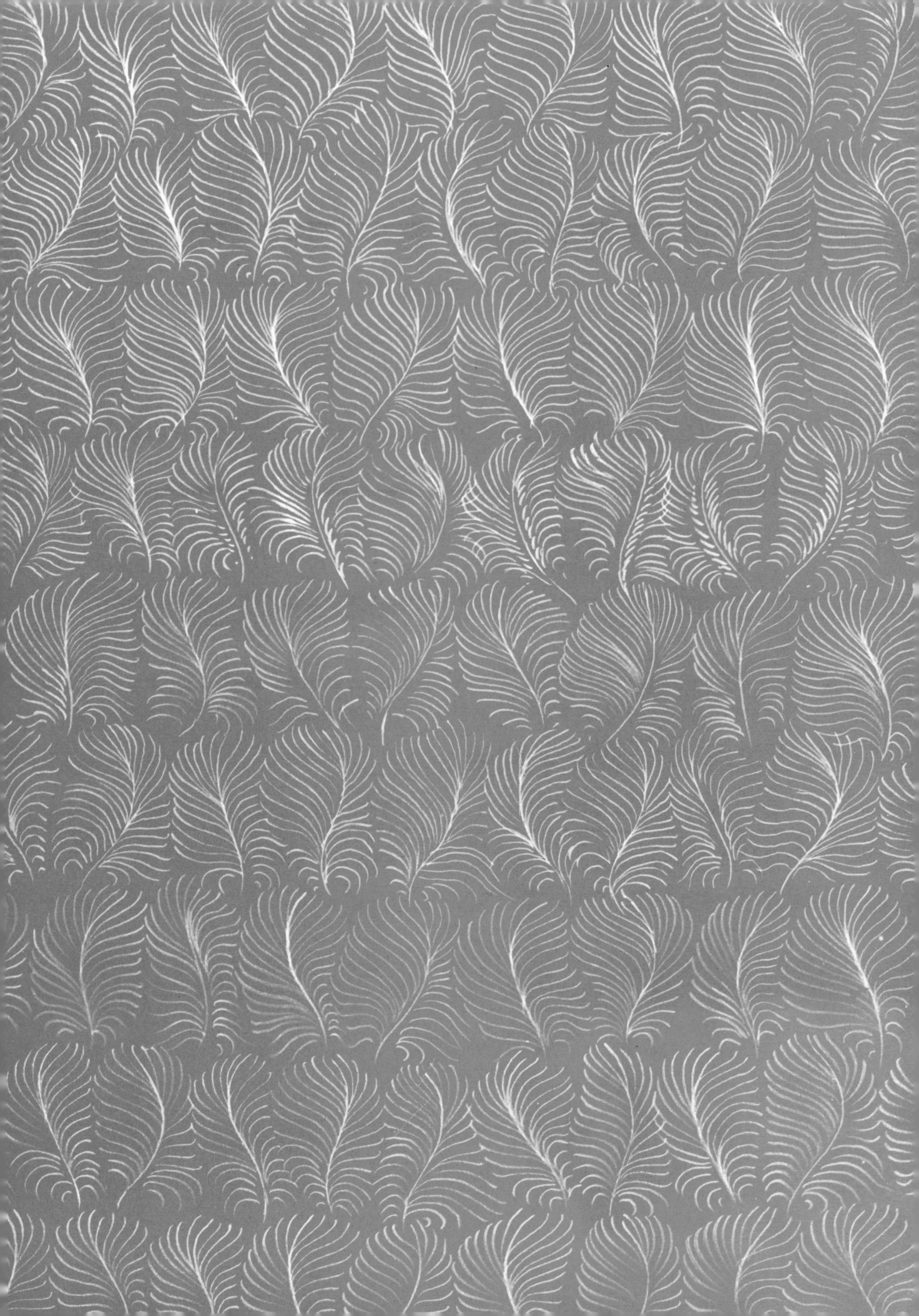

UHU

Annette Macarthur-Onslow

ALFRED A. KNOPF : NEW YORK

First edition 1970, reprinted 1973

Text and illustrations Copyright © 1969 by Annette Macarthur-Onslow.

All rights reserved under International and Pan-American Copyright Conventions.

Published in the United States by Alfred A. Knopf, Inc., New York. Originally published in Australia by Ure Smith.

Printed in Hong Kong.

Library of Congress Catalog Card Number 67-28120.

For F.L.K., his best friend

T 7004291

'Without supernatural assistance, our fellow creatures can tell us the most beautiful stories, and that means *true* stories, because the truth about nature is always far more beautiful even than what our great poets sing of it, and they are the only real magicians that exist.'

King Solomon's Ring
    by Konrad L. Lorenz

FOREWORD

The story of Uhu (pronounced yoo-hoo) was brief but devastating. He came and went, between May and September, like a feather on a puff of wind . . . upsetting our whole existence, grubbying the furniture, rearranging the house, and temporarily banishing the cat (unlike the characters in the song, our owl and pussycat did *not* agree).

He had no one to show him how an owl should behave, and therefore his antics, though sometimes funny and touching, were always full of purpose.

He taught us that, contrary to common belief, owls are not all fierce, impersonal, predatory creatures; they also like company, like having their heads scratched, and chirrup with pleasure when their ears are tickled. It was shortage of information about keeping tame owls that prompted me to write this little book. Had I known then what I know now, Uhu might have survived a little longer and might even have gone back to his wild state and lived a normal life.

Perhaps, one spring day, you too may find a baby owl like Uhu. (Owls of his kind quite commonly fall out of their nests in old conifers or hollow woodland trees.) If so, you may learn something from Uhu's story, and I hope that your bird will be as good-natured, friendly, brave, clownish, wily and inventive as Uhu, although, I hope, a little less prone to trouble.

For Uhu it was bound to be trouble from the start. He was one of the inquisitive ones who must tempt providence. There he was on the ground, having fallen out of his nest in the pine tree... a defiant white ball of fluff with enormous black-currant eyes and tiny beak clicking a warning to anyone daring to enter his territory among the roots and pine needles. For a creature born to inherit the forest this was all most humiliating. No doubt if I had not come along, a fox would have found him and made a hasty meal.

His old home bristled above him: inhospitable, spiky-dead branches. There was no apparent nesting hole for an owl among the branches, so he must have come from somewhere much higher up beyond the curtain of greenery. Could such a small bird have fallen all that way without being hurt? Why couldn't he straighten his legs? I picked him up gingerly, expecting a fury of beak and claws to tear at my fingers, but the little fellow was too tiny to grip properly and far too shocked to fight.

Buddi, who was sculpting in the cottage garden on the edge of the woods, took one look at him and said, 'It's a Uhu!' (That very day we had found that 'Uhu' was the German name for an Eagle Owl.) Uhu wasn't an *Eagle* Owl, but the name seemed to suit him, so Uhu he became.
All this time Uhu, quite frantic with fright, lay motionless on the grass with flies clinging to his tightly shut eyes. There were no broken bones or marks from his fall, so having decided that he was only shamming dead, we set about making a straw nest in a box to cheer him up.
The straw worked like magic. Uhu fussed and nestled in it. There was just enough room for him to move around. But there was nothing to stop him from falling out again, so we searched and found the perfect cage, a garden sieve that fitted over the box and kept out the flies as well.
For the first week, until he learned to open his mouth, Uhu was force-fed tiny pieces of meat in the semi-darkness of the tool-shed.

Towards the end of the week we found him trying to stand in his box. Off came the sieve and up jumped Uhu, squealing and flapping his tiny wings.

At this time Uhu stood about six and a half inches high and was, we supposed, nearly two weeks old. He was fluffy white and speckled with tiny brown, waxy feathers. His cheeky face with its forward gaze had an almost human expression. He wore outsize, wispy white 'petticoats' which he preened with care, bending his head to bat his blue eyelids with their fluff-tipped lashes.

In our unsettled condition, keeping a little wild bird was going to be terribly difficult. We couldn't take him on our hundred-mile trips to London. We couldn't leave him to fend for himself. We simply had to give him away before we became too attached to him.

Friends who had a country house near London were interested, and their rambling garden would be just the thing for an inquisitive owl.

Buddi cut holes in the lid of a cardboard box, and after this was fitted over Uhu's own straw-lined box, we drove to London with a very wide-eyed little bird. Every time the car door banged he clicked his beak and burrowed deeper into the straw. We learned that the *click* was Uhu's alarm, the noise of fear or warning. The *chirrup*, varying in volume, expressed either anger or pleasure, while the *squeal* meant just one thing: 'Fooooooood!' Everyone who saw Uhu was 'delighted' and 'enchanted,' but no one wanted the responsibility of looking after him. Not even our friends with the country house. So we kept him, feeling deep down that it was, after all, the right thing to do.

Back in the cottage Uhu began to discover what he could do. He was learning to stretch, learning what wings are, finding that feet are enormously cumbersome and have long unmanageable claws. (He didn't yet know that an owl's feet are his most useful asset for catching prey.) He sat in the grass moving his toes. Each foot had a reversible toe that could move either forwards or backwards.

Suddenly he was moving his feet, step by painfully slow step, towards the tangle of stalks in the old cottage rosebush. There, settled among the plants and insects, he sat looking out in the half-light.

At first we thought that, being a night creature, he would be blind in daylight, but we soon realized that his sharp eyes and ears were following the flight of birds and bees and the droning course of aircraft overhead.

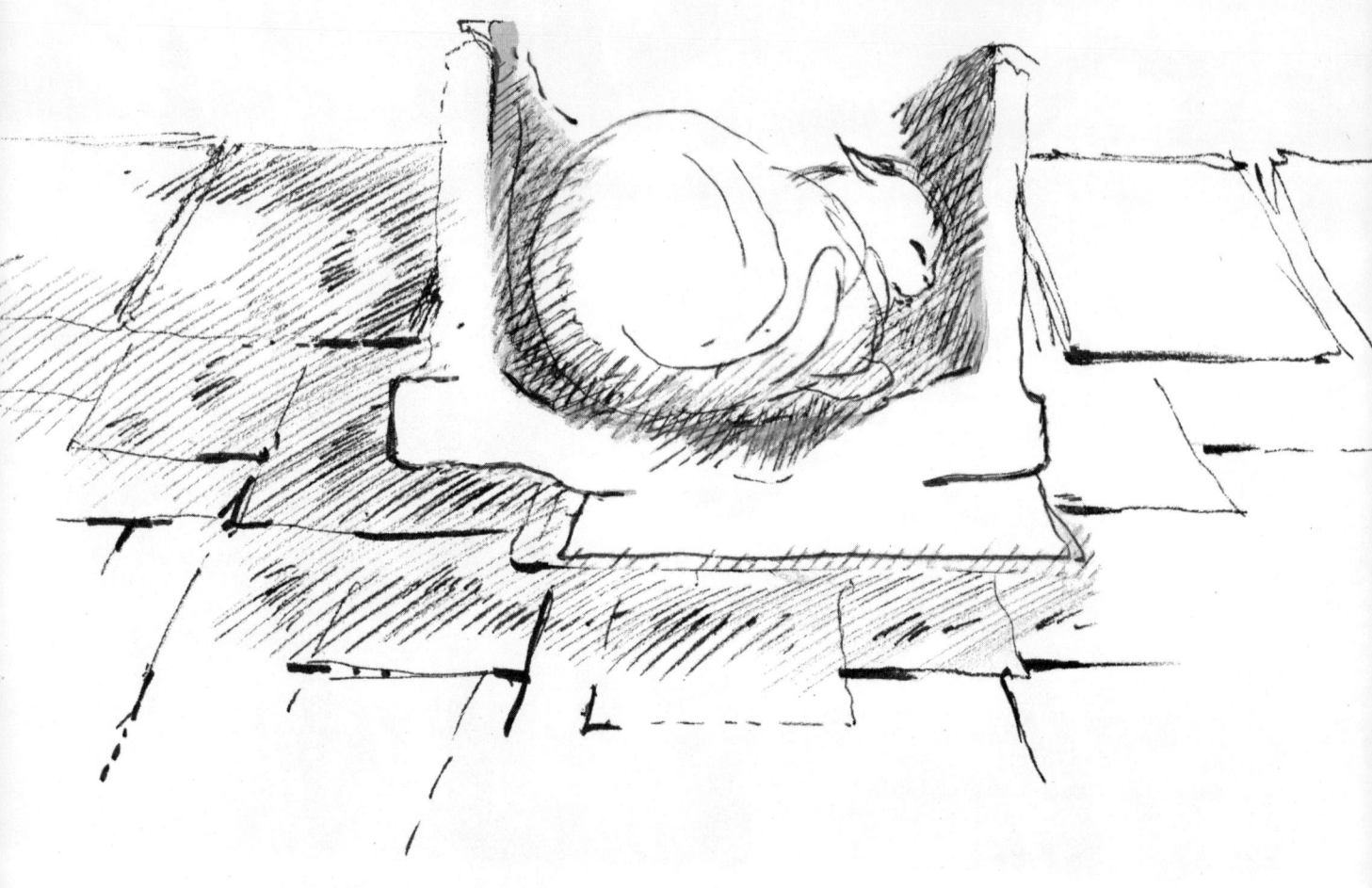

When we brought his box into the warmth of the house, Minnie the cat, who had ruled the roost for seventeen years, took one look, made a wry face, and went on strike.

On the first day she removed herself to the most inaccessible place, a small niche on the shed roof, where she sat looking thoroughly cross. She would have nothing to do with us until night came and she wanted to be helped down.

On the second day I found her deep in the woods, a place she braved only in moments of extreme provocation. After dark she returned as far as the studio (the halfway stage of her private entrance into the house). Here, for as long as Uhu was in residence, Minnie stayed, took her meals, slept and sulked!

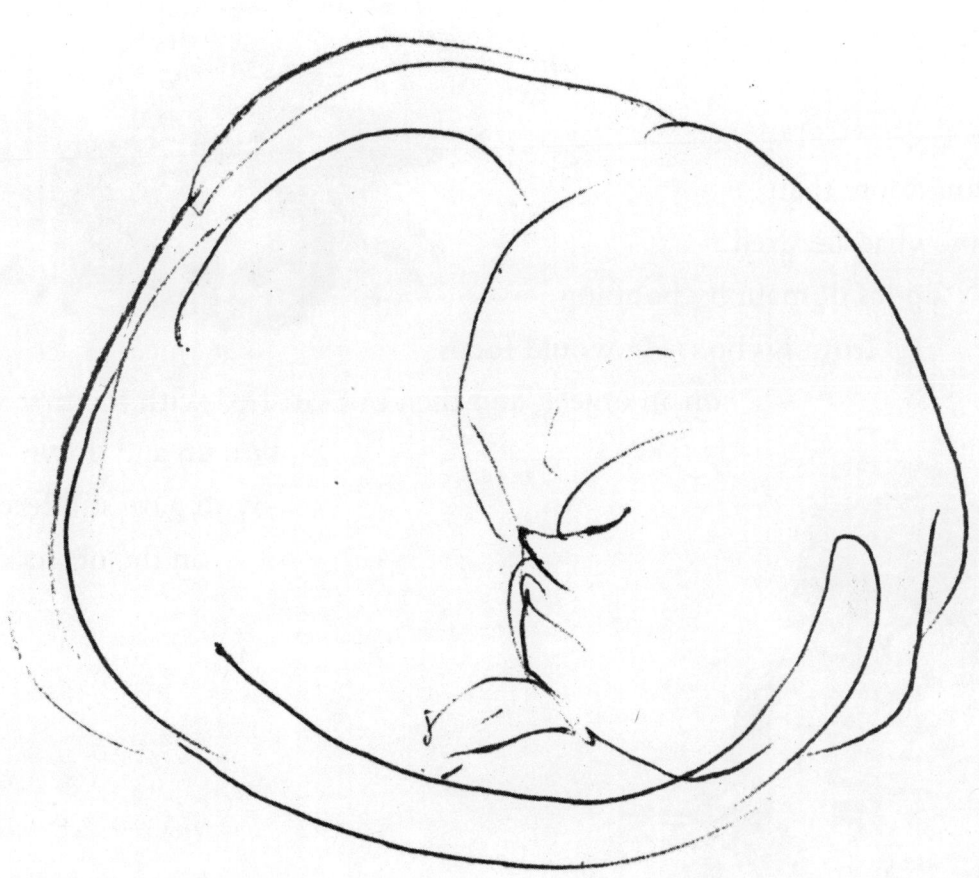

Uhu took over his new home with all the vigorous investigation that must have caused him to fall out of his nest in the first place.

Wobbling more than somewhat, he sized up his domain by bobbing from his box. He would focus on an object, and then not satisfied with the first view, bob up and down with gaze still fixed on the object . . .

side to side and round and round.

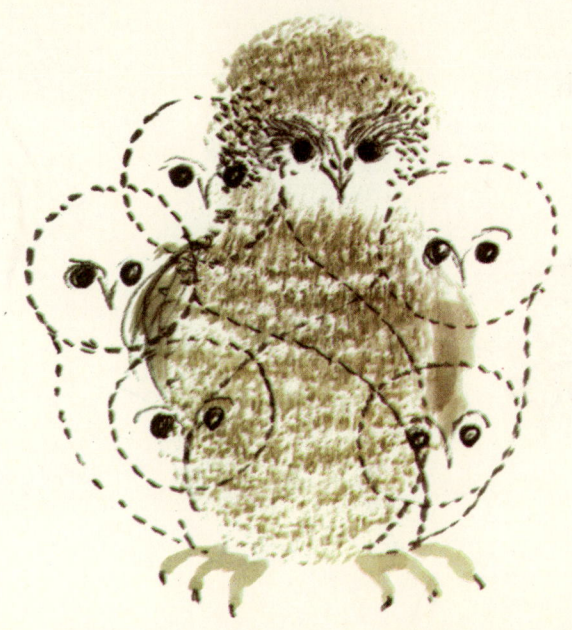

He could also swivel his head through 180 degrees and see equally well behind and in front of him.

Uhu's exercises included the 'one-way' and 'two-way' stretches.

From being a round, fat puff-ball, he would suddenly become tall and thin with two long legs and one long wing. This was the 'one-way' stretch.

The 'two-way' stretch meant
bending forward in a deep bow
and stretching both wings over
his head like a heraldic eagle.
He seemed to grow with every stretch.

He had already outgrown his old box, so Buddi made him a new one with a perch at one end and a hood at the other. It looked like a medieval cradle. Uhu loved this box. While the perch was still too wide for him to grip, he would stand rocking drunkenly in the middle of it. Quite suddenly he would flap his wings, plunge into the straw, bury his head and fluff up his tail, sometimes falling asleep just like that.

Uhu was a born clown. He loved to exaggerate, and took particular delight in showing off on the paper spread around his box. The box stood on an old and rather awkward bed. In two hops Uhu would be out of the box and onto the paper, where he would stand for several moments, brooding. Then slowly his ritual began, with concentrated wing-flaps growing faster and faster as he worked up to the climax, four steps backwards, a flip of the tail and hop . . . a squirt landed just within bounds. We expected him one day to overstep the paper and fall off the bed, but he always calculated perfectly.

Uhu's every move had to be planned. He took 'compass bearings' lengthwise, crosswise and in circles before setting off on his short woolly stumps with 'hands' behind his back.

Climbing was not so simple, especially as he always aimed at the highest possible point. It took a great many steps, and then all the bobbing and bowing in the world could not save him from a final scramble.

The day Uhu met his first prey he was feeling rather pleased with himself because he had just made his first big jump onto the garden seat. There in the sun were five blue plastic bags waiting to be 'caught and killed.' Uhu took them on, one after the other, shaking and tearing them like a dog worrying a rabbit.

When he was four weeks old (by our calculation), we bought a bird book to learn more about him. One picture showed five fluffy owlets sitting on a branch—all unmistakably Uhu with their black eyes (other owls had vicious pale eyes). So Uhu, according to our book, was a Tawny Owl (or a Brown, Grey, Beech, Ferry, Hoot, Hooting, Ivy, or Wood Owl). 'Tawny Owls make the nicest pets,' said our book. We could expect him to twitter or chirrup until autumn, when his voice would change to the ringing 'Kwick-kwick-OO-OO-OO-OO' (the cry described in fairy tales as 'To-wit-to-woo'). Remembering the magic nights of autumn, when the air was full of these calls, we could hardly believe that our twittering, squeaking, comic little bird could ever utter such sophisticated sounds.

It was June and a late spring, as lovely as spring in Gloucestershire can be. The apple trees were laden with more blossom than I have ever seen, and the woods were full of bluebells, cuckoos and young deer. Uhu sat watching the bees in his rosebush, while we sat in the first warm sun.

One day, just as we were planning to leave for London, Uhu broke his leg! How it happened is a mystery. Uhu had been jumping busily in and out of his box, when suddenly he went toppling all over the place, squealing like a rabbit. We bundled him, box and all, into the car and off to London.

In London we called the zoo.
'We have an owl with a broken leg, can you do something about it for us?'
'Madam, we're sorry about your owl, but we're doing a caesarean on a tiger this morning, you'll have to go elsewhere.'
'Well, can you recommend someone? It's important that we see him quickly.'

Eventually they referred us to some posh West End vets. *Osteogenesis-Imperfecta*... big words which imply brittle bones. This was how the vets described Uhu's condition. He had not been getting his calcium ration, and while his body had developed his bones remained like matchsticks.
The first dressing they put on slipped down. The second dressing, a plaster one, put pressure on the lower bone and caused a greenstick fracture. The third dressing was a metal splint. Bound with elastoplast, it covered the whole length of his leg, with a little metal heel to support the weight.

Uhu soon adapted himself to his gammy leg; he learned to kick it out in front of him and take most of the weight on the other leg. With undaunted spirit he clumped around like one stiletto heel on the march.

We became regulars at the clinic. All the Kensington ladies with their manicured poodles gushed over Uhu... 'Oh, isn't he the sweetest thing!'... Uhu just sat in the middle of the floor, staring at the dogs.

The vets prescribed calcium tablets and cod-liver oil with his meat, and London Zoo added cotton wool or fur (if we could get it) to the menu for roughage. One of the oddities of owl digestion is that they have to cough up pellets—little balls of this roughage—at least once a day. In the wild, nature would have provided Uhu with mice or rabbits.

Grass was an afterthought, a Uhu special. He would root for hours in the country, acting more like some bloodhound learning its hunting technique than a mere bird getting its ration of green stuff. When exhausted he would flop like a dog under the garden seat with his head pillowed on a stone. He was so carried away by this new sport that nothing could interrupt it, not even rain! One day we lost him during a downpour, and found him rooting, ecstatic and soaked to the skin. His fluff, sadly deflated, stuck out in wisps around his neck like the top knot of a Maribu stork. Without the fluff he resembled a scraggy chicken.

Uhu couldn't understand water at all, nor did he seem to need it. When I showed him some in a glass once, he went mad, putting his whole head in and getting water up his nose, then sneezing it out in small squirts. He must have thought the transparent glass would let water through the bottom, because he nibbled underneath the glass as well.

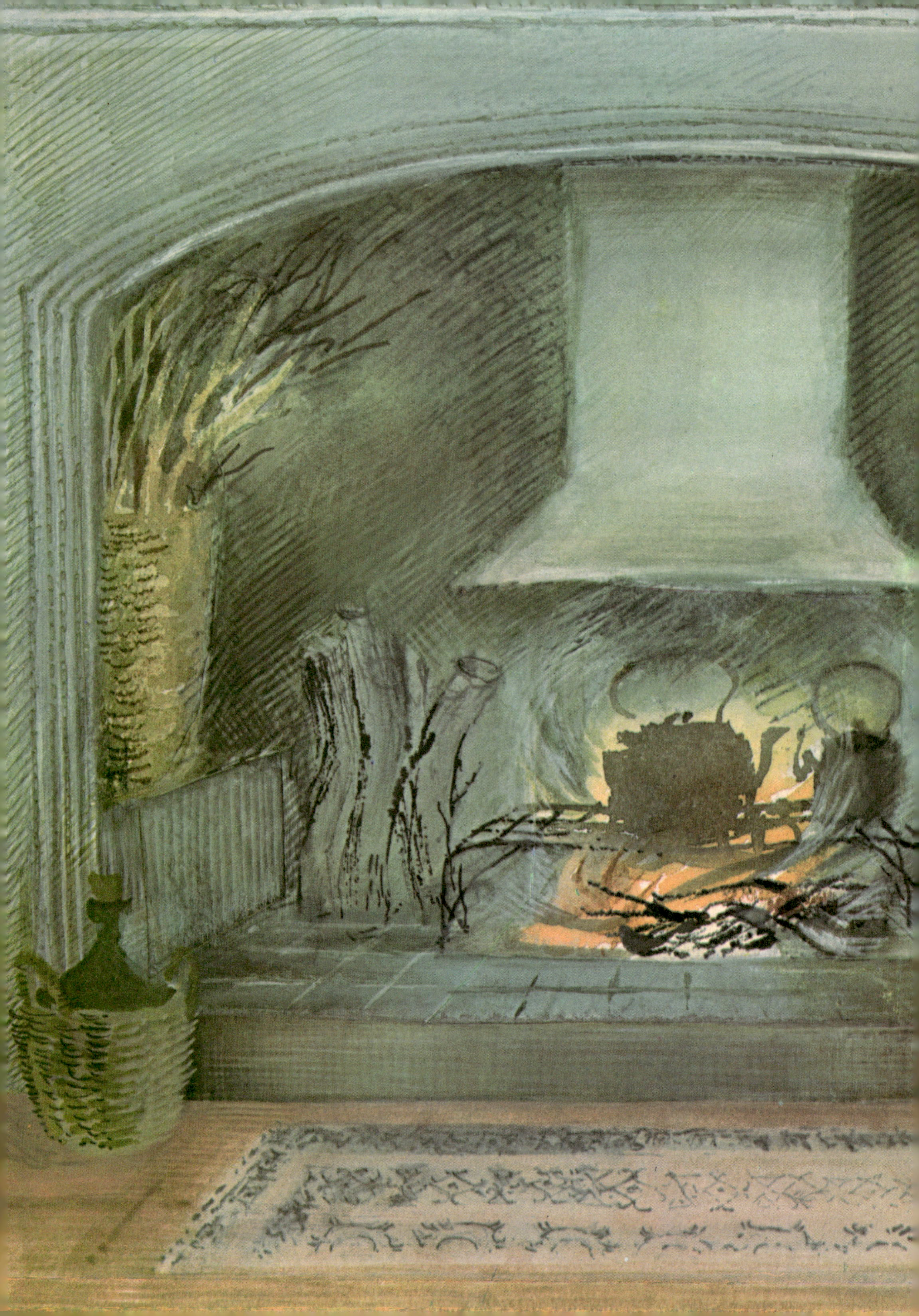

The first time he saw fire he hopped over and stood gazing into the embers like a cat. He was so fascinated that Buddi made him a bed on the little wall seat inside the fireplace. Fluffed and broody, Uhu nestled in the far corner of the seat. Then, quite suddenly, he wasn't nestling any more. In a fit of madness he had flown off the seat and was flapping wildly, stuck in the grill between two kettles and getting rather warm. His very first flight had nearly ended in disaster!

When an owl flies, his big soft feathers dampen the sound. It was a new sensation to have Uhu land on or near us when least expected. He was enjoying his first taste of power, the power to be (sometimes) thoroughly annoying. Many mornings I awoke to find him perched on a chair across the room, staring as though willing me to wake. It was too late to close my eyes again. With a plop Uhu would land on my feet, my knees, my shoulder – whichever point happened to be highest. Once he tried to land on my head!

Uhu thought it was a great game when I fumbled for an old laundry bag and threw it over my bed as protection. He would dodge the bag all over the bed; one morning he even flew off the bed with it, 'conquered and killed' it on the floor, and dragged it under a chair, clawing, flapping and tangling with the legs and crossbars.

He was always up to something. There was the time he woke me with a terrible noise. He had jumped into the waste-paper basket and was wedged tight, flapping wildly, treading the contents, and only just tall enough to reach the rim and hang on.

Another morning I found him hanging upside down like a bat, caught in the landlady's lace curtains.

He was transfixed by the wonders of the dressing-table mirror. That bird in the foreground was without question himself. But in the background, who could that be, appearing in two places at once? He bobbed to my reflection, then back to me, back and forth, back and forth.

Glass in any form completely mystified him. One night, standing in the cottage window, he spotted something outside, something that he wanted to investigate. Smack! He hit the window pane! Bump! He was back on his bottom! Smack! Bump! Smack! Bump! He tried again and again with appalling loss of dignity.

If he sometimes made a fool of himself, he was more often made a fool of by us.

He came on shopping expeditions to London, nestling in a basket while groceries were piled in beside him, suffering untold miseries in crowds, riding on strange smelly buses.

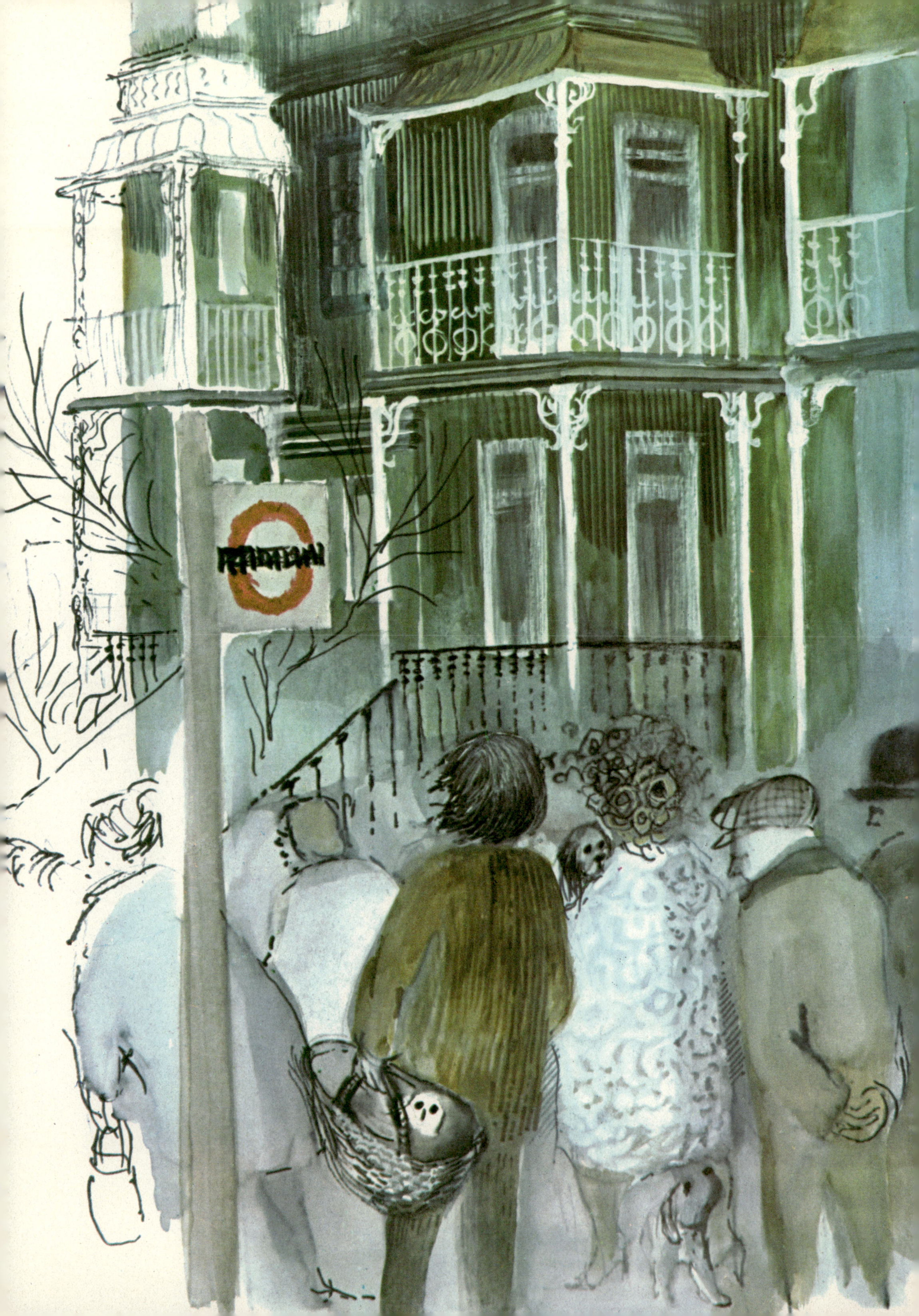

He also came visiting, exploring each new place with maddening enthusiasm. When he met a goat-skin rug that belonged to our friend Stod, Uhu leaped from his basket and challenged the rug to a fight that ended in a clean draw. Next he met a cat called Rover who eyed him sideways across a rush mat. Rover's owner, Meg, thought that Uhu should have a key in his side to wind him up, and Rover must have said something as rude as his mistress' thought, for Uhu suddenly fluffed himself up like an angry Prairie Owl, and Rover vanished instantly.

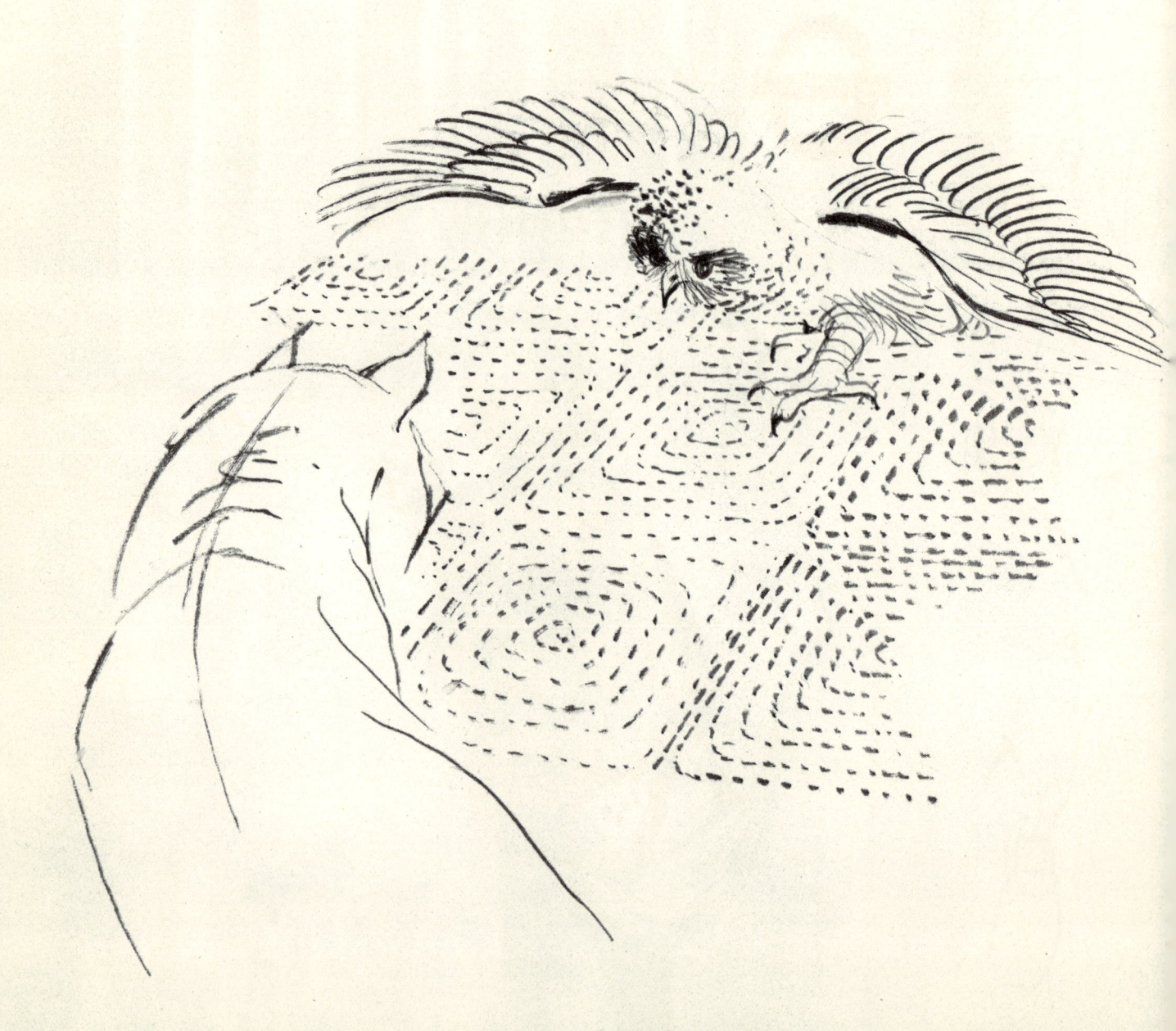

Then he met a fascinating box of colored pencils belonging to Dinah. Standing on the pencils to watch her draw, Uhu forgot himself and dirtied Dinah's work. He had to be taken home in disgrace.

After that I followed him about with a newspaper on all visits. Uhu was very indignant. His droppings were his only anti-social habit, a habit that was impossible to break because a bird cannot be spanked like a puppy.

Uhu suffered the buses, the crowds and the strange peering faces good-naturedly. He had already accepted us as 'owl kind' and played along with us, courteous, confused, but never passive. He was, I suppose, what we would call a good sport.

Poor crazy mixed-up Uhu! No one could tell him that an owl is normally an anti-social, lone-hunting night bird. Our owl craved company so much that he followed us everywhere. Long before he could fly, he had even scrambled upstairs, beak over claw.

Occasionally a whisper from the wild reached Uhu like a note on a passing wind. He might be standing at a window watching sparrows, when suddenly he would go all hawk-like and eerie. Then the moment was over and he was the woolly, twittering infant once more.

It seemed we were his only friends. Cats hated him, dogs mistrusted him, and worst of all, he was stormed by birds. When Uhu sat under his rosebush the garden was all a-chatter.
Uhu looked quite unconcerned and precociously wise for such a junior owl. He would perch like this for hours, particularly if there was some activity going on. One of his best-liked roosts was a bale of scrim that Buddi used for sculpture. Here Uhu would sit, gently rocking himself, watching the master at work.

With July came the fall
... the fall of baby-fluff.
White tips flew everywhere, and the waxy
sheaths protecting his
new, reddish-brown
feathers showered like
scales whenever he shook
or preened himself. Where
the vet hadn't shaved
them, his fluffy white
'petticoats' hung in sad
wisps, like overgrown
wool. New herringbone
feathers sprouted around
his face and a light russet
down appeared on his
blue eyelids.

His decidedly reddish
tinge all over meant,
according to our book,
that 'he' might be a 'she'
after all. Well, to us, 'she'
remained 'he.'

Baby-fluff

Breast feather

Tail feather

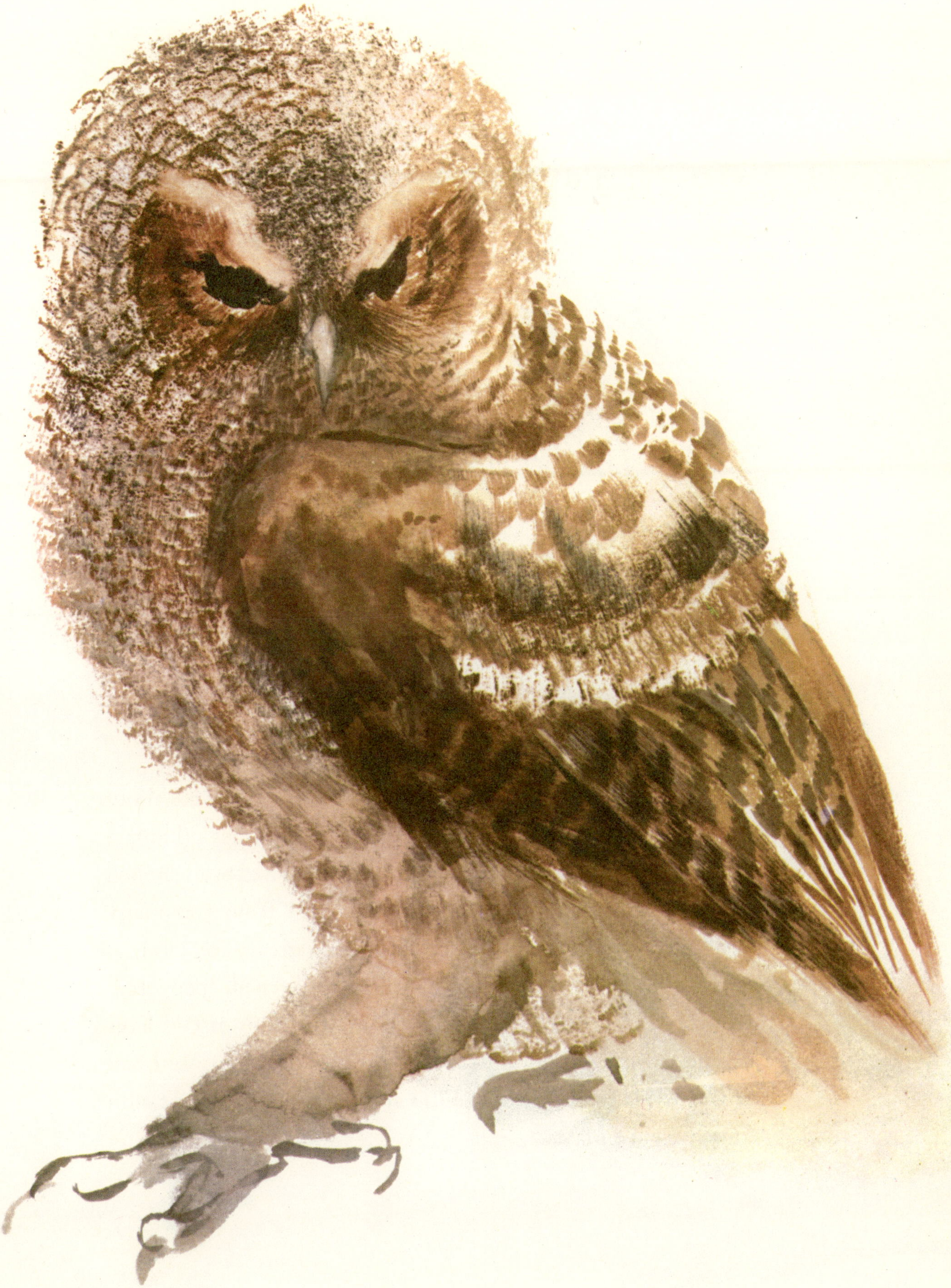

As Uhu changed and grew, his appetite grew too. He ate about one quarter pound of chuck steak a day, or sometimes a (luxury) wing of chicken. We had heard of one owl that had been choked by raw liver, and of another that had died from too many garden worms. Sausage, we found, was too greasy for Uhu, so steak or chicken it was: sliced, lean, or moistened, 'peppered' with calcium, ground and bound with two drops of cod-liver oil, and garnished with a pinch of cotton wool. By now I had refused to play nursemaid to Uhu any more and let him ration himself from a plate.

Feeding time was a great game. The tiny pieces of meat had to be hunted down and 'killed.' One day he carried the battle too far and jumped onto the hearth, swinging his tail into the fire. This cost him three tail feathers.

In August we went abroad. Uhu and all his paraphernalia — his box, his tablets, his cod-liver oil and cotton wool went to stay with our friend Colin.

Colin had a Squirrel Monkey called Kosh, whom Uhu had already met. It had been a dubious first meeting. Kosh sat chained to the back of a seat, his delicate face and ears wiggling over a strawberry clutched in tiny hands. Uhu, looking more than ever like a fluffy toy, turned his head away from Kosh for one second...

grab! A tiny pink hand shot out and pulled his tail. There was a loud squawk from both of them, and in a flurry of feathers Uhu was on the floor.

We could picture Colin's studio, full of maquettes, paintings, stuffed animals and antique furniture, becoming a complete chaos over the next month. But to our surprise, Uhu and Kosh became great friends, and sat together for hours on end conversing in squeaks and squawks.

Both small animals had been alone in the world of human beings. Now, as each met a creature of similar size, the effect was electric. They became almost inseparable. Yet Kosh must have caused further confusion in Uhu's small mind and made him even less sure of his identity.

At last the day came when the splint was removed from Uhu's leg. Up until this time we had hoped that he would one day learn to fend for himself and become a proper owl, but now our hopes were dashed. The leg was horribly stiff and deformed. Uhu would always be a cripple.

As if in a wild bid for freedom, Uhu was flying, flying with a vengeance. Nothing was safe, least of all Uhu. He flew high, veering sideways like a drunkard (minus three feathers, his 'rudder' was cock-eyed) and landing heavily on his gammy leg. To make matters worse, he took up residence on top of a cupboard.

We thought seriously of putting him in a cage, or clipping his wings to retard his flight until his leg was stronger.

We visited the zoo to see how the Uhus there tolerated their cages. They all seemed well fed and rather sleepy... owls of every description from the perky little owl to the great white Snowy Owl with its feathery workhorse feet. The Tawny Owls peered at us from their perches, turning their heads rather than their bodies, as owls will. There was a pair of Tawny Owls (the elder one was about twenty-five years old) beautifully marked with little russet darts running down their fronts. Contemplative, sleek and bored. We couldn't imagine our inquisitive Uhu existing in a cage like his fat relatives. So we left him with Kosh to continue his indoor aerobatics.

Some weeks later Colin called to say that Uhu had broken his leg again. He had fallen on the same leg, but this time the vet, a new vet, shook his head. 'That'll never mend properly,' he said. 'However, I'll do my best for you.' So once more Uhu found himself in a splint, flapping and trying to stand.

In human terms he had a broken hip. (Owls don't have real hips, but this break had the same effect on his anatomy as a hip break, that is, a general collapse of the 'undercarriage.') A human being in this state would have been bedridden for some time, but Uhu, being Uhu, fought and struggled to get on his feet. Naturally the more he struggled, the more he panicked, and the more he panicked the more he collapsed.

We shut him away in a room by himself, away from Kosh and other disturbing influences. Here, stacked up on cushions, with his bad leg comfortably propped up, we tried to make life bearable for him, for poor Uhu was rapidly losing interest; his feathers were becoming battered and disheveled by his struggles. The vet gave him a new brand of calcium, with vitamins added to pep him up, but Uhu just flopped around like a broken moth.

As long as he flapped and fought, we knew that the old spirit was hard at work, the spirit that had pulled him through many crises before. There seemed no reason why he shouldn't pull through again. But the day came when Uhu stopped struggling and just lay quiet and still. At first we thought that he had learned some common sense and was at last letting nature take its course. Then we realized that something was seriously wrong: Uhu was dull-eyed and listless. He swallowed a little food with difficulty, and barely responded to having his ears tickled. Days went by while he lay, hardly eating, growing weaker and weaker. Then he refused to eat anything.

Placing him in his old straw-lined basket, we put him in the car and sped off to see the vet. Uhu was lying quite still, face down in the straw. There were the intolerable moments of waiting—waiting at the traffic lights; waiting for someone to cross the road, a bicycle here, an old lady there; waiting at the vet's door; waiting in the office, frantic for every precious moment. At last the big kind hands lifted him from the basket and set him down on the table.

Such treatment usually met with a barrage of abuse and wild flapping, but today the little bird lay still and silent. The vet examined him and shook his head. Uhu, our resilient fighting Uhu, was dead.

Exactly what caused his death puzzled the vet; he thought Uhu had probably been pining. Pining for what, we wondered. For Kosh? For us? Or was it an inexplicable longing for his wild state?

We laid him in a little box and buried him under his favorite rosebush. It was autumn now, and the garden, so often a-chatter when Uhu was there, was strangely silent.

Minnie appeared, cautiously testing the air. Then convinced that all was clear, she stalked into the cottage and settled herself by the fire. It was heartless of her to be so unconcerned, but then Minnie is a cat, and after all, cats don't like owls... and it used to be her cottage.

The next night as the moon rose, the woods echoed with the cries of the first Tawny Owls of the autumn. Poor Uhu... he never knew what it was to be a real Tawny Owl and call in the trees.

Next spring we knew there would be new Uhus, many of them ... and perhaps if we walked often enough in the pine forest we would one day find another little white ball of fluff with black-currant eyes, clicking its beak under a tree.

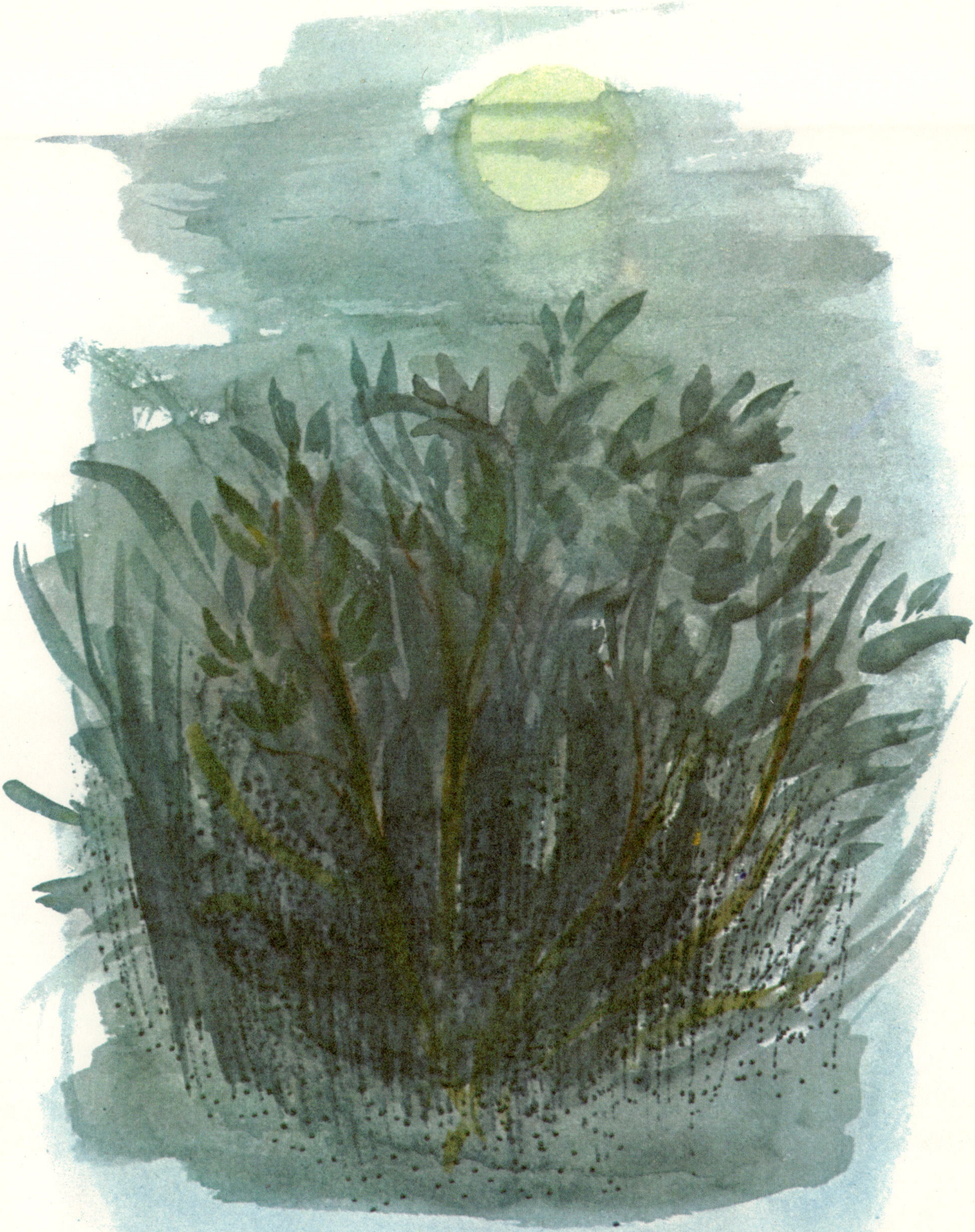

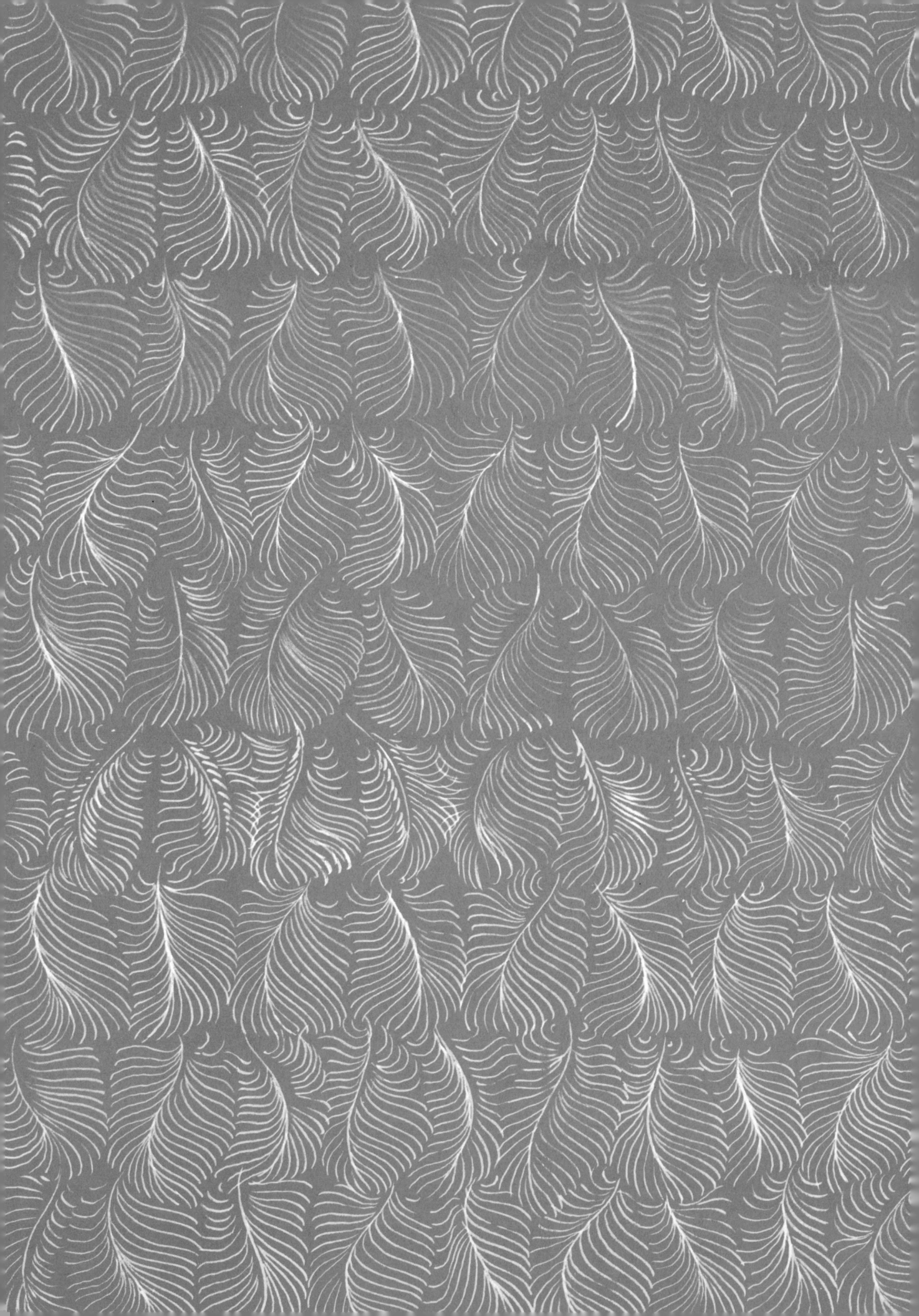

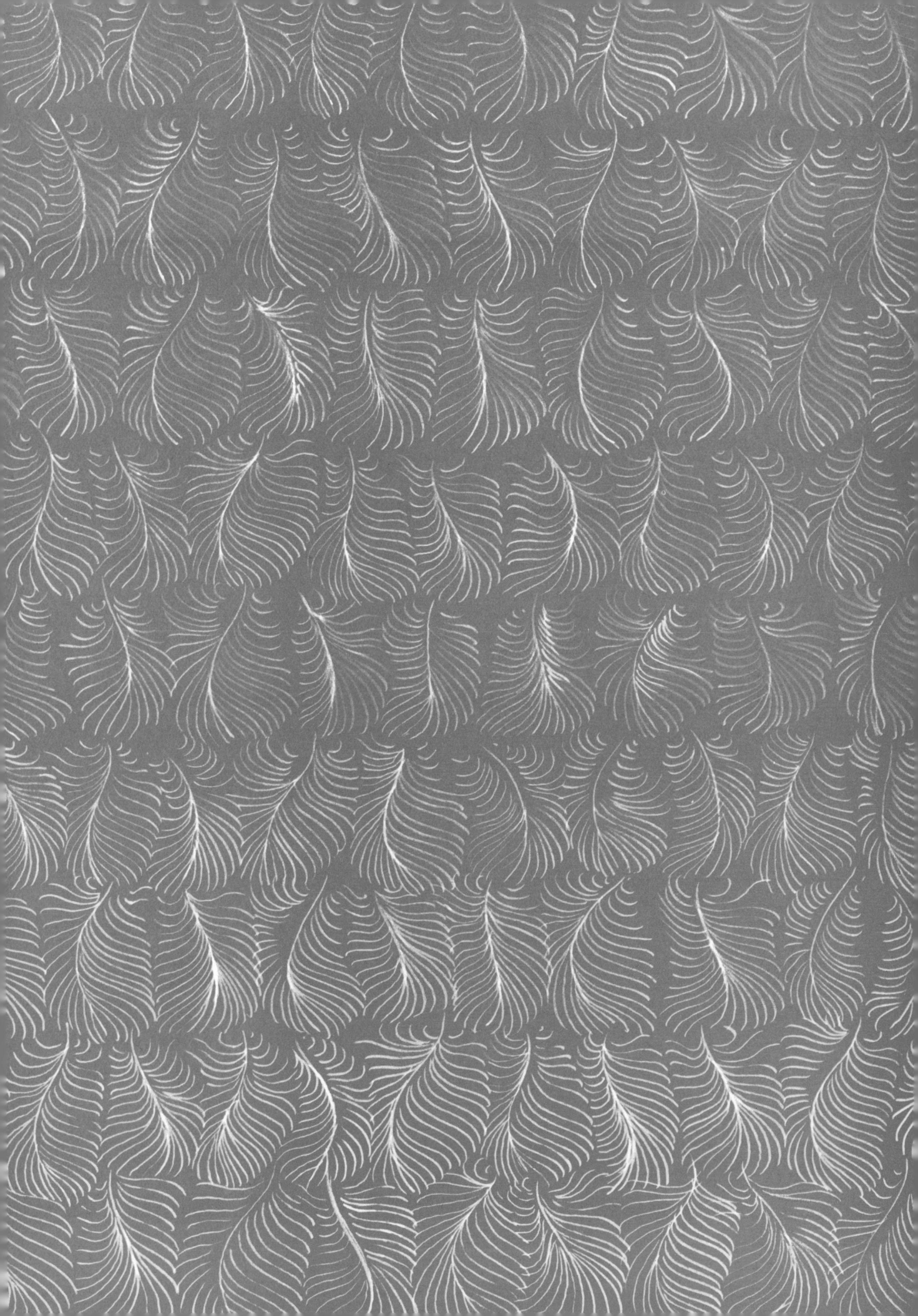